Published by Creative Education
123 South Broad Street, Mankato, Minnesota 56001
Creative Education is an imprint of The Creative Company

Designed by Stephanie Blumenthal

Photographs by Richard Cummins, Joe McDonald, Mary Ann McDonald,
Tom Stack & Associates (W. Perry Conway, John Gerlach, Thomas Kitchin,
Mark Newman, Brian Parker, S. K. Patrick, John Shaw, Dave Watts),
Unicorn Stock Photos (Rod Fergason, Tom McCarthy), Viesti Collection
(Luca Tettoni, Robert Winslow), Ingrid Marn Wood

Library of Congress Cataloging-in-Publication Data

Nieson, Marc.
Elephants / by Marc Nieson.
p. cm. — (Let's investigate)
Includes index.
ISBN 1-58341-194-1
1. Elephants—Juvenile literature. [1. Elephants.] I. Title. II. Series.
QL737.P98 N54   2001
599.67—dc21   00-064496

First edition

2 4 6 8 9 7 5 3 1

Smart Apple 5/03 16.95

ELEPHANTS

MARC NIESON

Creative Education

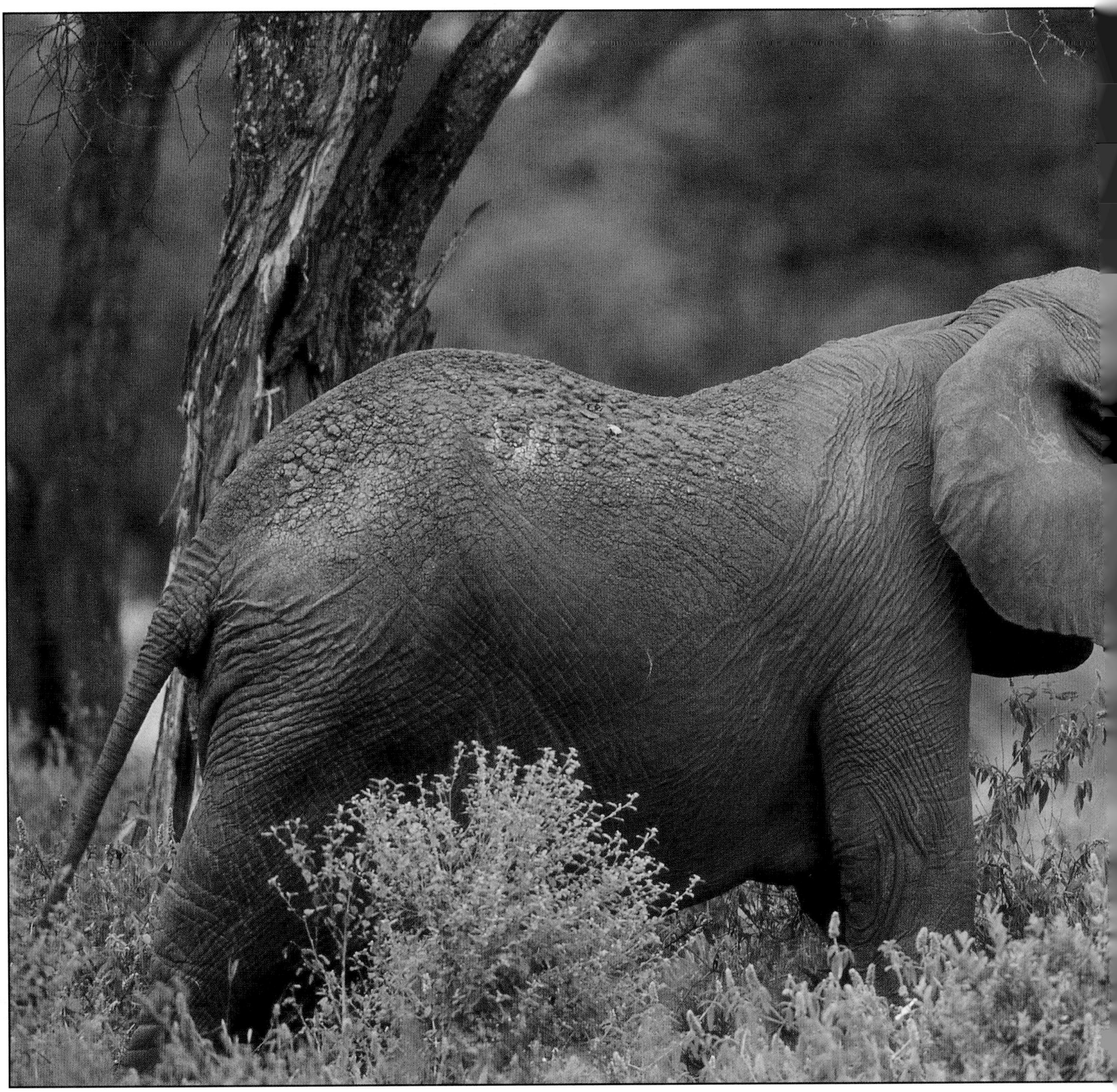

Of all the animals that walk the earth, the elephant is by far the largest. Only certain kinds of whales are more massive, and only the giraffe stands taller among land animals. Elephants have the biggest ears of any animal, and their tusks are the largest of teeth. The mighty elephant looms large not only in the animal kingdom, but in human fascination as well.

ELEPHANT
FEET

The bones of an elephant's foot are permanently on tiptoe. Underlying fatty pads help the elephant support its weight and walk almost silently, without leaving tracks.

5

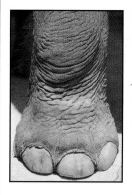

Above, the foot of an African elephant
Left, an elephant uses its trunk to reach food

ELEPHANT
TUSKS

Only two-thirds of an elephant's tusk is visible. The rest is embedded in the bone of the elephant's skull.

ELEPHANT
TRUNKS

An elephant's trunk measures about five feet (1.5 m) long and weighs about 300 pounds (136 kg).

The tusk and trunk of an African elephant

Perhaps the elephant's most distinctive feature is its huge nose, called either a proboscis or a trunk. Modern day elephants come from an ancient line of long-nosed mammals called proboscideans (pruh-bah-si-DEE-ans). The first proboscideans were about the size of a pig and lived in northern Africa 50 million years ago. Over the ages, hundreds of distant ancestors to the elephant **evolved**, but they all became **extinct**. Mammoths and mastodons are the best known of these. They were like today's elephants in size but were more solidly built, with hairy bodies and longer, curving tusks. Scores of mammoth fossils have been unearthed across the globe, from tar pits and sinkholes in the United States to the frozen **tundras** of Siberia.

Today's elephants are either African or Asian. As a rule, African elephants are larger than Asian elephants, but the size and shape of their ears offer a better way of telling them apart. The African elephant's ears are extremely large. They fan back over the elephant's shoulders and are shaped like the continent of Africa. The Asian elephant's ears are about half as large and are shaped like India. African elephants also have lower, sloping foreheads. An Asian elephant's forehead is high and bulges into two humps.

ELEPHANT
E A R S

Elephants spread their ears out wide when they are angry or afraid. Because of their size, they fear few **predators**. *Their enemies include lions in Africa, tigers in Asia, and humans.*

7

An African elephant charging an intruder

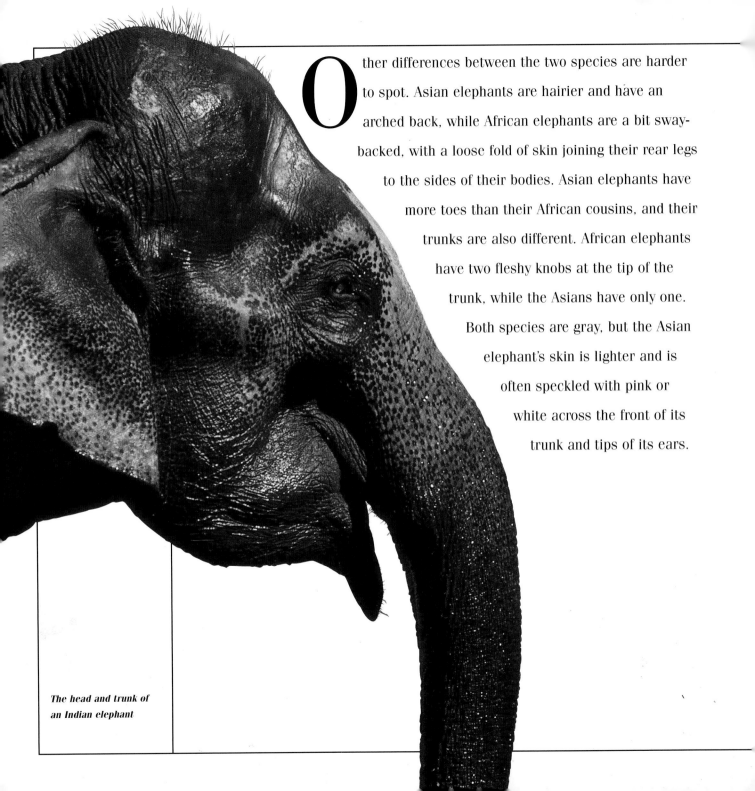

Other differences between the two species are harder to spot. Asian elephants are hairier and have an arched back, while African elephants are a bit sway-backed, with a loose fold of skin joining their rear legs to the sides of their bodies. Asian elephants have more toes than their African cousins, and their trunks are also different. African elephants have two fleshy knobs at the tip of the trunk, while the Asians have only one. Both species are gray, but the Asian elephant's skin is lighter and is often speckled with pink or white across the front of its trunk and tips of its ears.

The head and trunk of an Indian elephant

Full-grown African elephants weigh five to six times as much as a car.

Above, an African elephant feeding Left, African elephants cooling themselves at a water hole

A̲ll elephants live in tropical countries, where climates stay warm year-round. African elephants are found south of the Sahara Desert, across savannas, jungles, and swampland. They can be divided into two sub-species: bush African elephants (*Loxodonta africana africana*), which are more widespread and numerous, and forest African elephants (*Loxodonta africana cyclotis*), which are considerably smaller and inhabit the denser rain forest regions in central and western Africa. Male bush elephants are the largest of all elephants, averaging 11 feet (3.3 m) in height at the shoulder and weighing around 13,000 pounds (5,900 kg). The female bush elephant can reach nine feet (2.7 m) tall and weigh 8,000 pounds (3,600 kg).

ELEPHANT
S K I N

An adult elephant's skin alone weighs up to 2,000 pounds (907 kg).

Above, the skin of an African elephant Right, young Asian elephants on the move

Asian elephants inhabit areas of southern and southeastern Asia, dotting isolated forests and jungles in a dozen different countries. On the mainland, the Indian elephant (*Elephas maximus indicus*) is the most common subspecies. Males measure 9 to 10 feet (2.7–3 m) tall and weigh upwards of 10,000 pounds (4,500 kg); females measure eight feet (2.4 m) and weigh about 6,600 pounds (3,000 kg). Other Asian elephant subspecies are found on the island nations of Sri Lanka and Sumatra.

ELEPHANT BODIES

In some ways, elephants are similar to humans. They are warm-blooded mammals that nurse their young, have hair, and generally live from 50 to 70 years. However, because of their great size, they need huge areas of land to roam and graze, lots of natural shade, and large bodies of water.

ELEPHANT
FAMILY

The elephant's closest living relatives are the manatee (an aquatic mammal that looks like a walrus) and the hyrax, which is about the size of a rabbit and looks like a rodent.

Above, a manatee, or sea cow
Left, a rock hyrax

ELEPHANT
SHOWERS

Elephants protect themselves from sunburn and insect bites by showering themselves with earth.

S taying alive in the hot and harsh **equatorial** landscape is no simple task. Elephants have adapted in amazing ways to survive. Their dry, wrinkled skin is often a full inch (2.5 cm) thick, which protects them from thorns and broken branches. In fact, another name for an elephant is pachyderm (PACK-i-derm), which means "thick skin." This tough hide is very sensitive, however, especially to insect bites. Elephants have no sweat glands, either in their skin or anywhere else. To stay cool in the tropical sun, they seek out shade, roll in the mud, or flap their great ears, which lowers their body temperature.

African elephants cooling themselves with a dust bath

13

Elephants have amazing teeth. Their ivory tusks are actually long, curved upper front teeth. Tusks are permanent and continue to grow throughout the elephant's life, sometimes exceeding 10 feet (3 m) in length. Elephants use their tusks to dig for water or salt and to uproot or take the bark off trees. Their tusks can also be used as weapons. The elephant's other four teeth are each about the size of a brick. They are replaced by new teeth six times over the course of the elephant's life and wear down from grinding so much coarse food—between 300 and 600 pounds (136–272 kg) each day.

Above, baby elephants have no tusks
Left, an older elephant has long tusks

ELEPHANT
THIRST

An adult elephant can suck up nearly four gallons (15 l) of water in its trunk at a time. Elephants need to drink around 40 gallons (151 l) of water per day.

Above, an elephant bathing and drinking Right, an African elephant using its trunk to gather food

The elephant's remarkable trunk is a combination of nose and elongated upper lip. It is extremely flexible and strong, and elephants use it to gather and lift food, grasp, carry, toss, scratch, hug, warn, trumpet, sniff, suck, shower, and snorkel. It can lift anything from a single blade of grass to huge logs. The tip of the trunk is very sensitive to touch, and the sense of smell is **keen**. Elephants rely mostly on their senses of smell and hearing, since their vision is poor.

ELEPHANT
SNIFF

Elephants raise their trunks to sniff the air and are capable of catching scents from as far as five miles (8 km) away.

15

Mud caked on the skin protects elephants

ELEPHANT
TRUNKS

The elephant's trunk has more than 40,000 individual muscles and tendons that allow it to bend in all directions.

Above, an elephant's trunk is flexible Right, two African elephants greeting one another

Elephants also use their trunks to communicate. They greet and speak to one another with gestures and sounds. In recent years, scientists have learned that elephants use low-frequency rumbling sounds to communicate, even when they're miles from each other. These sounds are too low for humans to hear. When elephants are close together, they can convey many of their feelings by simply shifting the positions of their heads, ears, or tails.

ELEPHANT
BABYSITTERS

Although an elephant calf is nursed only by its mother, one or more other females, called aunts or allomothers, will babysit.

ELEPHANT
ETIQUETTE

From 1665 to 1681, an African elephant lived at the French royal court of Versailles. It drank one and a half gallons (5.7 l) of wine each day.

Right, young elephants are never left unprotected Far right, two young males fight for dominance

ELEPHANT FAMILIES

Elephants are extremely social animals and live in highly structured family groups. A typical family consists of 5 to 15 related adult females (called cows) and their young. The oldest female, called the matriarch, is always the leader. She determines the group's migrations for food and water. Often the families in a region will band together loosely, forming a large herd.

Each hair on a mature elephant's tail is as thick as a standard pencil's lead.

An African elephant's tail

A dult males (called bulls) live more solitary lives at the outskirts of these families. Young bulls leave their family groups when they're 10 to 12 years old. Sometimes a small number of males band together. Like the females, they also have a specific **hierarchy** and often challenge one another for dominance. Once each year, older bulls enter a special period called musth (MUST), when they're particularly aggressive and likely to challenge each other. Only the older, most dominant bulls mate with the females.

ELEPHANT
Y O U N G

Like humans, elephants grow up slowly. Calves can nurse for up to four years, although they begin eating grass and other foods when they are just a few months old.

20

Above, a young African elephant nursing
Right, baby elephants are very curious
Far right, babies stay close to their mothers

Much of the elephant's social life revolves around breeding and raising young. A female elephant can usually start reproducing around the age of 13, bearing a single baby (called a calf) every four to five years until she is well into her 50s. Her pregnancies last 20 to 22 months. Newborns can walk within an hour of birth. Nearly blind at first, they use their trunks to feel their way around. Adults are very protective of calves and will circle around them if they sense a threat.

...th
...ways
found ...ground,
ancient Siberian leg-
ends told of huge
rats that lived in the
earth. The word
"mammoth" comes
from Estonian words
that translate to
"earth-mole."

*Above, a "watch
out for elephants
crossing" sign
Right, Bhutanese
artwork depicting
an elephant*

ELEPHANTS AND HUMANS

Human interaction with proboscideans dates back to prehistoric times. Early cave drawings (some more than 17,000 years old) show detailed pictures of mammoths. These drawings have survived in such African nations as Zimbabwe, Chad, Libya, and Algeria, as well as in parts of France and Spain. Images of elephants grace our greatest cathedrals and temples, from Rajasthan in India, to Paris in France, to Angkor in Cambodia. Pictures of elephants have appeared in Hindu, Buddhist, and early Christian religious paintings. They show up in mosaics, on merry-go-rounds, and as cartoon characters such as Babar and Dumbo.

Humans have long celebrated elephants in the flesh, too. They were prized by Roman and Chinese emperors, Indian **maharajas**, Ashanti kings, and British monarchs. People of all ages, cultures, and classes have long flocked to circuses and zoos to see this giant mammal firsthand. Even today, at annual festivals honoring the elephant in Sri Lanka and Thailand, they are elaborately decorated, paraded, and even raced. Yet in no other country has the elephant been as revered and integrated into people's everyday lives of work, myth, and religion as in India. When they die, some working Indian elephants are draped with flowers and mourned.

ELEPHANT
HISTORY

In the year 218 B.C., Hannibal, a general in Carthage's army, crossed the Alps with 37 elephants to attack the Romans.

23

ELEPHANT
BELIEFS

The Marins, from Upper Myanmar, believe that the creator of the earth was an elephant and that the earth itself is the interior of an elephant's body.

A working Indian elephant in Jajpur, India

The first records of an elephant being tamed date from around 3500 B.C. Although never fully **domesticated**, elephants have been trained for use in warfare, hunting, transportation, and, of course, circuses. Their great strength and intelligence, and their ability to learn, has made them ideal for work in logging, construction, and agriculture. But to obtain elephants for work, zoos, or circuses, people have often used painful methods of trapping and training them. Many elephants have been mistreated, or have even died, as a result.

25

ELEPHANT
S T A R

The word "jumbo" comes from a popular circus elephant of that name who toured England and the United States in the late 1800s.

ELEPHANT
STRENGTH

An elephant's tusks can lift loads weighing as much as 2,000 pounds (907 kg).

Left, an Asian elephant in a circus act
Far left, Asian elephants using their strength to help loggers

ELEPHANT
SLEEP

Elephants don't sleep much. They take short naps while standing or lie down for a couple of hours at most. They also snore—loudly.

26

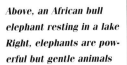

Above, an African bull elephant resting in a lake Right, elephants are powerful but gentle animals

By far the biggest threats to the elephant today are hunting, the demand for its valuable ivory tusks, and the spread of human settlements and farming, which have shrunk the elephant's natural **habitat**. The very survival of the world's oldest living mammal is now seriously threatened.

ELEPHANT
SPEED

Elephants walk three to six miles (5–10 km) per hour, but when angry or panicked, an elephant can sprint at 25 miles (40 km) per hour.

Worldwide conservation groups have helped draw public attention to the elephant's **plight**, but solutions to the problem aren't simple. In 1989, an international ban on the sale of ivory was passed, but already exceptions have been made. Many African and Asian nations have created special **reserves** for their wild elephant populations, but the reserves have a limited amount of land. When the elephant herd grows, there isn't enough food to support them all. **Poaching**, too, continues. Wildlife experts warn that it will take more than a few isolated reserves to save the elephant.

Above, a bull elephant in full charge
Left, an African elephant eating from the edge of a lake

ELEPHANT

Elephants tend to travel in single file and may cover 20 to 30 miles (32–48 km) a day walking to and from water holes.

Some elephant conservation ideas involve moving elephants to different habitats, establishing **corridors** so they can travel between reserves, and introducing birth control programs. In short, better understanding and management of elephant **ecosystems** are needed. Of course, more time is needed to conduct these studies—time that the elephant may not have.

A herd of African elephants crossing the savanna

ELEPHANT
SOCIETIES

The grassland tribes of Cameroon, Africa, have secret elephant societies. At special religious ceremonies, members dance wearing elephant-like masks covered with glass beads.

ELEPHANT
BRAIN

An elephant's brain weighs 11 to 13 pounds (5–6 kg), which is four to five times the weight of an average human brain and 1/800th of the elephant's overall weight.

ELEPHANT
BABIES

At birth, baby ele-
phants weigh around
250 pounds (113.5
kg) and are nearly
three feet (91 cm)
in height.

ELEPHANT
JUMPS

Elephants can't
jump—not even an
inch—but they can
stand on their hind
legs and are very
strong swimmers.

**Right, an African ele-
phant flapping its ears
to cool off
Far right, trainers make
holes in elephants' ears**

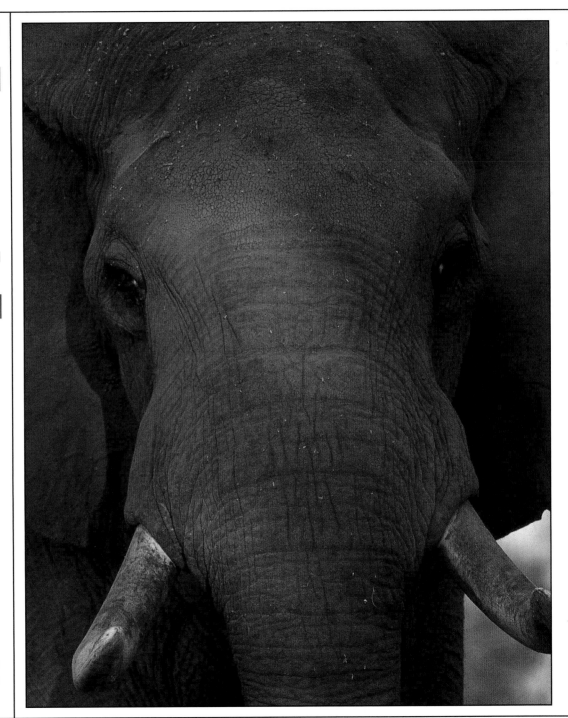

From as long ago as human history can recall, the elephant has been celebrated in life and legend. Preyed upon or prayed to, the elephant has always held our special respect and affection. Yet if the people of the future are to have more than just pictures and written memories of elephants, we must now work hard to protect and preserve these gentle giants.

Glossary

Corridors are narrow strips of land connecting two separate territories.

When an animal is **domesticated**, it has adapted to live with humans. Dogs and cats are good examples of domesticated animals.

Ecosystems are natural combinations of animals, plants, and their environments. The word emphasizes the ways they interact and support each other.

Land near the earth's equator is called **equatorial**.

Something that has **evolved** has changed slowly over time.

When the last animal of a species dies, the species is **extinct**.

The area where animals or plants live is called their **habitat**.

If a group of animals or people has a **hierarchy**, it ranks its members in order of their importance or power.

When an animal's senses are **keen**, they are extremely sharp.

Maharajas are Hindu princes.

A **plight** is a dangerous condition.

Illegal hunting or fishing is called **poaching**.

Animals that kill and eat other animals are **predators**.

Reserves are special lands set aside for animals to live on safely.

Savannas are grasslands with scattered trees and underbrush, either in the tropics or close to the tropics.

Treeless plains in the arctic north are called **tundras**.

Index